Love, Romance, and the Broken Heart

LOVE, ROMANCE, *and the* BROKEN HEART

A Collection of Poetry by
N. Jeffrey Blankenship

Illustrations by
Randy J. Blankenship

Photography by
Christopher Thompson

RESOURCE *Publications* • Eugene, Oregon

LOVE, ROMANCE, AND THE BROKEN HEART
A Collection of Poetry

Copyright © 2024 N. Jeffrey Blankenship. All rights reserved. Except for brief quotations in critical publications or reviews, no part of this book may be reproduced in any manner without prior written permission from the publisher. Write: Permissions, Wipf and Stock Publishers, 199 W. 8th Ave., Suite 3, Eugene, OR 97401.

Resource Publications
An Imprint of Wipf and Stock Publishers
199 W. 8th Ave., Suite 3
Eugene, OR 97401

www.wipfandstock.com

PAPERBACK ISBN: 979-8-3852-0658-2
HARDCOVER ISBN: 979-8-3852-0659-9
EBOOK ISBN: 979-8-3852-0660-5

VERSION NUMBER 01/30/24

LOVE

1. The Meaning of Love | 5
2. Hidden Treasure | 11
3. The Power of Love | 13
4. Conflict | 15
5. The Value of Love | 17
6. When | 19
7. The Cost of Joy | 20
8. When my Love | 22
9. Is it Love | 24
10. Wandering | 26
11. When love Lasts | 27
12. My Fall | 28
13. The Drowning of a Love | 30
14. The Illusion of Love | 32
15. The Root of Love | 34
16. Lost Love | 35
17. Wisdom | 39
18. Too Late | 40
19. Thawing a Frozen Heart | 43
20. Imperfect Love | 45
21. Love's Power | 46
22. Cherish | 48
23. Godly Friends | 50

ROMANCE

1. Clumsy Me | 55
2. A Single Rose | 56
3. An Intimate Kiss | 58
4. Love Built by Distance | 59
5. The Mortality of Love | 60
6. Truth | 61
7. Forever Quenched | 63
8. The Key to the Heart | 65
9. The Pain of Indifference | 69
10. When Two Hearts Connect | 71
11. The Deception of the Heart | 72
12. Places in the Heart | 75
13. Our Love | 76
14. An Offer of Love | 78
15. Forgiveness | 80
16. Just to Say I Love You | 83
17. The Tie That Binds | 84
18. A Resting Place | 86
19. Infinite Love? | 87
20. The Heart of a Man | 89
21. Never Another | 91
22. Love's Compelling Declaration | 93
23. The Measure of Love | 94
24. Light | 96
25. My Angel | 97

THE BROKEN HEART

1. Heart Cry | 103
2. If | 105
3. Pain | 106
4. The Purpose of the Heart | 107
5. The Masks We Wear | 109
6. The Yearnings of the Heart | 113
7. Too Late | 114
8. When a Heart's Been Broken | 116
9. Walls | 119
10. The Cruelty of Indifference | 121
11. The Lily | 125
12. Repairing a Shattered Heart | 127
13. Truth in Deceit | 129
14. Trusting God | 131
15. Trust | 132
16. Motives of the Heart | 133
17. The Wellspring of Motive | 135
18. Alone | 136
19. Justice in Love? | 138
20. The Heart Can be Evil | 140
21. Missing in Action | 141

PREFACE

Almost every man and woman, regardless of age or background, has felt love and has loved at some point in their lives. Sometimes love cannot be identified by the recipient and, at other times, the love seems so powerful, it is overwhelming. As a family law attorney for almost 40 years, I have witnessed the vast power of love's stronghold, as well as the devastation of its loss. The collection of poems in this book asks questions about WHY this happens, why love sometimes seems to thrive, and other times, it fails despite our best efforts to retain or revive it. These poems question our assumptions about love, romance, why hearts are broken and how a broken heart is permanently changed. These poems even question what love is and how different concepts of love may innocently shatter a heart. Love, Romance and the Broken Heart is an outpouring of the soul, a probing of the mind and an exploration of human expression.

ACKNOWLEDGEMENTS

I want to thank my wife, Nannette Marie, for the deep heart inspiration which led to the thoughts and expressions behind many of the poems in this book.

Thank you to my long time dear friend, Lisa Joy, for the multitudes of thought provoking conversations giving rise to the seeds for so many of these poems and for the many many times she encouraged me to create poetic expression for those thoughts.

Thank you to my dear friend and law school classmate, Rick Robinson, for his encouragement, patience, guidance and direction—as well as margaritas—in completing the final version of this book.

Thank you to my brother, Randy Blankenship and my son in law, Chris Thompson, for their talents and artistic input for this book.

Thank you to my son Jeffrey Adam Blankenship and my daughter, Erica Blankenship, for their willingness to engage me in deep discussions about the thought process behind many of the poems in this book.

And thank you to my amazing assistant, Amy Stewart, for her diligence, creative input and hard work in organizing, compiling, and completing this work. Without her assistance, this work would not have come together.

CHAPTER ONE

LOVE

LOVE

1. The Meaning of Love | 5
2. Hidden Treasure | 11
3. The Power of Love | 13
4. Conflict | 15
5. The Value of Love | 17
6. When | 19
7. The Cost of Joy | 20
8. When my Love | 22
9. Is it Love | 24
10. Wandering | 26
11. When love Lasts | 27
12. My Fall | 28
13. The Drowning of a Love | 30
14. The Illusion of Love | 32
15. The Root of Love | 34
16. Lost Love | 35
17. Wisdom | 39
18. Too Late | 40
19. Thawing a Frozen Heart | 43
20. Imperfect Love | 45
21. Love's Power | 46
22. Cherish | 48
23. Godly Friends | 50

THE MEANING OF LOVE

Where does love come from?
Why does it grow?
Is it more than a feeling?
More than something we show?

Is love just a decision?
A mere act of the will?
Mustn't the heart be involved?
Or would not love remain still?

For though the mind might coerce
Our bodies to strive,
Can not only the heart
Constrain a soul to life?

With our cognitive thoughts,
Our limbs we can raise,
But will common mobility
engender an embrace?

Isn't the passion of the soul
A requisite sense?
Can mere logic arouse fear
For protection and defense?

Can cognition alone
Inspire relief from aggrievement?
Or is the fount of emotion
Compelled for bereavement?

Does victory alone appear
From the quality of one's facts?
Or is such inspiration found
In the spirit's aspiring attacks?

Does enactment of thought
Change, grow and bend?
Or is it not restricted to
Merely achieve its end?

For a decision alone,
It seems to me,
Can never become more
Than what it began to be.

So if, with the mind alone,
One cannot passion beget,
Must we then say that
Love must passion forget?

Can a lifelong decision
Without passion survive?
Or from mere will alone
Can passion derive?

My cognitive logic
Screams in derision
That passion never comes
From only a decision.

No, passion is austerely
An act of the soul;
It cannot be found
Apart from this goal.

So, is love more than
A decision to act?
Is it more than a feeling?
What is the fact?

True love requires
An act of the soul,
An entrenched desire
To be made whole.

To be united with one
Whose personhood completes,
Realized only by the passion
Of the soul in each heartbeat.

But true love cannot rely
On passion alone,
For emotion stems from
flawed flesh and bone.

True love must be both—
The will and soul united.
A feeling of passion
Yet also action decided.

For commitment alone can
Human emotion's waves ride
But only passion arouses desire
To be by your love's side.

HIDDEN TREASURE

Since the dawn of mans' creation,
Through piracy on the seas,
Men have hunted hidden treasures,
Some pearl they can seize.
Wealth and fortune to attain,
Fulfillment for the soul.
So why then does the search go on,
After man achieves that goal?
Did the treasure so hard fought for
Fail in its satisfaction?
Did that treasure ever quench the thirst,
Or was it parched with stupefaction?
Did that treasure fail to astonish,
Falling short in its benefaction?
Did it fail to encroach the parameters of
Effectual distraction?
For when man searches for an answer
But fails to understand the question,
The answer which he ultimately finds
Accomplishes mere repression.
For if treasure were the answer to the
Heart's most profound uncertainty,
Then the search would yield contentment,
Satisfying all perversity.
But that it woefully falls short,

Never approaching the optimal solution,
Then asked was that in error,
To the human condition, pollution.
For that which satisfies the soul,
That of hidden treasure,
That which cannot be held,
Nor can it be measured,
Must be pure, essentially real,
genuine and true,
Yet for it, there's sacrifice to feel—
A cost that must ensue,
For that which gratifies the soul,
The heart's life-giving blood,
Is sadly rare, like mystery,
It's called unfailing love.

THE POWER OF LOVE

Is love a creation of the heart
to which the mind reacts?
Why then is love so victimized
by logical attacks?
Is the heart swayed by emotion,
While the mind relies on facts?
But not also must the spirit
Lift up and extol?
Isn't a man the fruition
of body, mind and soul?
Are not every one of us
triune beings for infinity?
Is not love itself designed
to endure for all eternity?
Perhaps then could that fact
Be the root of love's fragility?
But why then does love's magnetic force
Draw irresistible such affinity?
Its power like a raging storm
overwhelms the logic and spirit,
So mighty is its compulsion,
Some have even come to fear it!
Yet its drawing strength is innate,
Its dominion is so firm,
What influence then do we fear?

To disavow or to affirm?
Can humanity resolve this riddle?
Can a man resolve his guilt?
Or will passion assure his acquittal?
Is that how love is built?

CONFLICT

When the instinct of the heart
Clashes with the mind,
Which inclination should prevail?
Is there some way to find,
Apart from a crystal ball,
Which of these instincts to assail?
All decisions must be weighed
On those facts which are known,
But should feelings from the heart effect?
Should they ever control?
Which is truth?
Which is right?
Knowledge or passion,
Or forfeit the plight?
The heart and the mind,
Both elements of the soul,
But when they struggle and conflict,
Which is supreme for the toll?
Which has the sensitivities to comprehend?
Which has that innate sense?
On which one should a man depend?
To reconcile that conflict intense?
How can a man know if the heart is wrong?
When those instincts could possibly err?
Does the heart ignore the truth,

Supplant with fantastical flair?
Or does the mind disregard all passion,
Stripping all emotion to bare?
How must a person reconcile,
Transcending the heart and mind,
Searching for the truth,
Until they finally align?

THE VALUE OF LOVE

What mystical quality was designed the heart to fill?
Does the heart have the capacity to submit to love's own will?
For if true love has its place,
To fill a void in the heart,
Can there ever be too great a sacrifice,
Love's satisfaction to impart?
For if true love has its cost,
How can one measure
Fulfillment of the soul?
Is there any cost too great
To make the heart eternally whole?
But is true love is ever 'meant to be',
Is there some celestial plan?
Some enigma that we cannot see,
Hidden treasure since creation of man?
Or is love simply random fate,
Nothing to see but mere chance?
No plan, no pattern, no grand design,
Just purely circumstance?
Yet if the latter were the rule of the day,
Then would the seed of passion have no role to play?
Does not instinct and wisdom plant in our mind
Logic which prevails over being intellectually blind?

And if our hearts and minds are designed for the truth,
Do we not have instinct for love's intrinsic way?
And once we find it deep in our hearts,
what price for love then would we pay?

WHEN

When is love the satisfaction of life?
When will the stars fill the night ?
When will eternity last forever?
When will the eagle take flight?
When will the storm create ocean waves?
When will the sun warm the earth?
When will the warrior be true and brave?
When will a mother give birth?
When will music alone write the song?
When will Heaven be pure?
When will death cause sadness?
When will real love be sure?
When will genuine love be true?
When will love compel sacrifice?
When will love feel fresh and new?
When will love alone fulfill life?
Is genuine love forever true?
Does it ever divide, not unite?
If true, then "always" is the key,
For true love knows no twilight.

THE COST OF JOY

What is the source of joy to the soul?
Does joy have a cost?
Is there a toll?
Is joy a decision to be content?
No tolerating dissent,
No room for lament?
Can the mind dominate the heart?
Is the heart the master or slave?
Can the will compel joy to reside,
Cast out discouragement,
Instill the brave?
So what facet of a man
Comprises the heart?
Why does it exist,
Does it purpose impart?
Or in mindless flight, can it be expelled,
Superfluous indeed,
No utilitarian purpose,
Like a life choking weed?
Or is the heart that nebulous swallow
From which abundance flows,
Without which life is ever hollow,
Despondence to expose?
So are the satisfactions of the heart
Worth the heavy cost to be paid?

For its sorrow, loss and even despair
Deliver cuts from the sharpest blade.
Or is joy far too exorbitant,
Too costly to absorb the tariff,
The heart then must be banished,
dispelling its celestial seraph?

WHEN MY LOVE?

I know that my heart will beat again,
Someday when the oceans are dry.

I know that I will love again,
Someday when I stop asking 'why?'

I know I won't hear the memory of your voice,
When the sun refuses to shine,

And I know that my heart will forget your gaze,
When memories are no longer mine.

But when will my lips forget your kiss,
And my hand your tenderest touch?

When will my arms no longer yearn
To hold and caress you so much?

When will my soul forfeit its desire to
Feel the warmth of your smile?

And when will my heart restore and be whole,
Happiness an unknown domicile?

I will cease to feel the soft of your skin,
Someday when the stars lose their shimmer.

And I know I won't sense the radiance of your eyes
Someday when my heart has no quiver.

Your name will not stir the calm of my soul
Someday when the moon hides its face,

And my heart will not break with the cry of your tears,
Someday when God exhausts all his grace.

My heart longs for your embrace,
My eyes yearn to see your face,
My body craves your tender touch
And my soul desires your being so much.

To you, I am starved to express my love,
To comfort your sorrow with love from above.
For a love so strong as the one we share
Can only come from the Creator's care.

For there is no other person nor any possession,
That can rival my love for you, my obsession.
I will dream, think and pray for you eternally,
And my love for you will thrive in the sweetness of eternity.

IS IT LOVE?

How can a man know if he is in love?
How does he know if it was sent from above?
Sometimes a love can happen so fast;
So how can he know if it will last?
Infatuation is merely a moment we feel,
Pure physical attraction,
no spiritual seal.
Love has to be more,
More than we see
Or what we can touch,
For love sets us free.
Freedom is always bought with a price,
So love must be costly,
Requiring sacrifice.
Will mere infatuation warrant that gamble?
Won't that soon burn out,
Like the wind blows out a candle?
For infatuation is passing,
No foundation to give it strength,
It is far far too fragile,
Though it may first burn intense.
So when does a man know
if this love is true?
Will he bear the cost?
Will it his spirit rescue?

Must he control or possess?
For if so, this love will oppress.
Love and freedom exist hand in hand,
It will not own, but always give.
Love will draw, you understand
By the freedom it offers, but never a captive.
Will love ever make demands?
For are concessions from mandates gifts?
Is a gift expectant ever of commands?
Or will it always uplift?
A true genuine love expects nothing to receive,
But yearns always to devote.
It's only solace in human truth
Is that for which it hopes.

WANDERING

Can a love become lost?
When it cannot find its way?
Where it may struggle for direction,
But feels so led astray?
Or perhaps was it never lost,
But simply running to hide?
From pain and hurt that squandered it,
From the tears that it had cried?
If love is lost, can it seek to find
The bread crumbs that mark the trail?
The steps that must be followed,
To find the fairy tale.
Or is it destined to the abyss,
Where hopelessness prevails?
Love no longer to conquer all,
Awaiting hope to assail.
Can the forest become so deep,
The trees expand so tall,
The thorns so sharp and dense,
Love has no hope at all?
Does hopelessness then strangle love's last breath,
Its withering life to take?
Must love then succumb to death,
For love and only love's sake?

WHEN LOVE LASTS

What quality love will ever endure?
What will make it last?
Can a person predict if it will die?
How wide is that net cast?
If it is true and if it is real,
How can it deepen and grow?
Does it matter how deep that love feels,
How deep in the heart's soil is it sown?
For enduring is more than just emotion,
It must be more than mere passion.
It must involve ever fiber of the soul,
It must exist in the soil of compassion.
Compassion, regardless the spin of the globe,
Compassion, to cultivate empathy.
For a love to endure, hearts must merge,
And then strive to love endlessly.
Emotions will pass.
Feelings will change,
They run their cycle and diminish,
But the flow of the heart,
Lasting and strong
Can never be assuaged to finish.

MY FALL

I knew that you'd be busy
So you couldn't take my call
But I wanted to leave a message
And tell you about my fall

Well, you see that I'm not hurt—
Not a broken bone in sight.
I guess you could say I'm lucky
Even if I'm not too bright.

By now you're probably wondering
What on earth am I rambling about?
It sure doesn't sound like an injury
To make me worry, fret or doubt.

No— I didn't break a bone,
Tear the flesh or cut the skin.
I didn't strike my arm, my knee,
My head, my foot or shin.

Yet my fall left me helpless,
Unable to fight back or to battle.
This fall took me by surprise,
And knocked me off my saddle.

My fall caused my heart to falter,
Never bruised but sometimes blue,
For the fall that has turned my life around
Was when I fell in love with you.

THE DROWNING OF A LOVE

Does a love ever descend beyond the abyss?
Too deep in its transcendence to find it?
Too cold it has grown from long time remiss,
Where darkness imposes a blindness?
Drowning beneath the stormy billows,
Buried in the seabed's sand,
Can it ever be recovered?
Or will it expire, obscured from the strand?
Like an anchor with a broken chain
Sinking to fathomless chasm,
Can a drowning love still search for air,
Or is living a mere phantasm?
Has hope for its breath
On the surface remained?
No life giving droplet
For which it has strained,
All indicia of survival
Having finally been drained,
By death's harrowing grip
Now is it constrained?

Shackled by surrender's futile desperation,
Has it forgone all its value
Expelled by indifferent evisceration?
Will it finally surrender the battle,
No longer death's threshold
To balance and straddle?
What power now remains
To persevere to inhale?
Or will love finally succumb,
It's demise to prevail?

THE ILLUSION OF LOVE

What if love is a game our minds play;
It cannot be defined,
A solution for life's decay?
So perhaps love is an illusion,
To navigate life's way,
Perhaps the heart's creation,
Solace for our dismay.
For man attempts to describe love,
By the way that it reacts
Like the wind we cannot see,
By motions that adapt.
But no many can define
What it means to love,
To feel, to care, to cherish.
For every man's ideal survives
While others have to perish.
If love is not absolute,
Lacking boundaries perceived,
Then is that fact not proof
That love's whatever we believe?
And if love is subjective,
Uncertain even aggrieved,
Then is love nothing more than
The mind's effort to deceive?
A comfort in the chaos,

Joy in the midst of grief,
A companion to share with us
Affinity to reprieve,
Serenity in the turbulence,
A fantasy the heart conceives?

THE ROOT OF LOVE

Once a love has vanished,
Can any effort make it show?
If the roots of that love have died,
From what could it ever grow?
All growth must have a foundation,
And love has a relational base,
But if the root surpasses creation,
How could that love ever efface?
So what is the root of a love
And how could it succumb to die?
Once that love has sprouted and grown,
Are not the roots too deeply entwined?
Can it expire quickly?
Or is time the author of death?
Does the answer even matter,
Once love has taken its last breath?

LOST LOVE

Some say it's better to have loved and lost
Than to never have loved before.
But it seems to me that
To have loved and lost is like shutting a once open door.
An open door through which one can smell
The fragrance of love's sweet rose,
An open door through which one can see
The beauty of love's pure glow.
The garden of love is alluring to all,
But so elusive to be found.
For everyone searches for a lifetime of love
And listens closely for love's true sound.
Craving so deeply in their hearts
The freedom that authentic love brings.
But it is so sad that few ever discover
The chime that love's bell rings.
Few ever sense the depth of its passion
Or feel its joy in their hearts.
Few ever know the changes love arouses
From the moment it starts.
So, Is it truly better to have loved and lost?
To experience true joy disappear?
Or perhaps is life sweeter when the purity in
True love never grows that clear?

For once having felt the joy that a genuine
True love creates,
Can life ever again seem full and complete
When love's garden has closed its gates?

WISDOM

When the spark has disappeared and
Cannot again be found,
When the flame has been extinguished,
And its flicker has no sound,
When there is no longer any fuel
With which to ignite an ember,
When the fury that once burned white hot
Cannot be remembered,
Has that fire any hope, burning from its remains?
Or has its life come to its finish,
Accept death to be humane?
Why struggle then to revive
That heart which no longer beats?
Does there exist some eternal hope
expecting reality to cheat?
For will the conflict not
a broken heart engender?
Or better still, would wisdom dictate
To Fate its final surrender?

TOO LATE

The crevasse of my heart was dark;
It was empty, it was quiet.
No sounds did it emit,
No voice did it acquire.
Was that heart alive or dead?
My mind wondered in lifeless peace.
For nothing in it long had stirred,
All feeling had come to cease.
Long ago had it resigned
To live without a mission.
It seemed that joy had made its exit,
Now its eternal condition.
Struggle as it had to find
That magic life giving elixir,
But rejection had long replaced
Rejuvenation's fixture.
The one to whom life had been given
Became the devil's toy,
Drawing each breath from this heart
With wisdom and stealth so coy.
Until life had given way
To a sad and relentless death,
This heart succumbing finally
Surrendering its last breath.
Is resurrection conceivable?

Can this heart ever breathe again?
Or is it relegated to lie in the tomb,
Death it's enduring domain?

THAWING A FROZEN HEART

Once in a while, a heart grown cold
From time and neglect, perhaps blame,
Can it find a spark, a flicker bold,
And endeavor to fan that flame?
Once that flame begins to burn,
Wider and farther its berth,
It starts to absorb that so cold heart,
And it begins to find new worth.
So that stone cold heart begins to warm,
As it thaws the ice surround,
The frozen tundra of its passion
Softening with the hardened ground.
Its innate rhythm fortified to resume,
Throbbing stronger as it warms,
Beats its music, newly attuned,
An ember burning in its core.
What is that igniting spark
Which starts this internal blaze?
What stimulus has the will
To melt the frozen glaze?
What truth in its spirit has the power
To so deeply internally pierce?
What voracious impetus can generate
Undying devotion so fierce?
What might can warm the base of a glacier,

Frigid to its marrow?
What power is so relentless
With vector intensity so narrow?
What virtuous supremacy exists
which can drive its arrow so sure?
What vigorous sanctity has capacity
So endless, and yet still so pure?
Only one essence can meet these demands,
Only one virtue to feel,
Only one truth a man understands,
Only one burden so real,
Only one quality a man can express,
Whether beneath or above,
Only one spirit that comes from the heart,
The spirit of genuine love.

IMPERFECT LOVE

Does a love live a finite life
And then perish from natural causes?
Is love a truly mortal emotion,
With victories, failures and losses?
If mere mortals possess capacity for love,
With all their inherent restraints,
Then why would we not expect love
To possess the same limits and fates?
Can flawed begat that which is perfect,
Create that greater than self?
Or does the creation bear all the marks
Of imperfect, traits of perfection dispelled?
Can the blemished envision the flawless?
Can the defective design the ideal?
How then would that which is tarnished,
In its issue its frailties conceal?
Can design transcend the designer?
Can finite evoke the eternal?
Can lead be made gold by the refiner?
Or is inherent nature too daunting a hurdle?

LOVE'S POWER

My love for you is like the wind.
It is present but it is not blind,
though at times it may not be seen,
Love is always manifested so kind.

But it also can be strong and powerful
Or silent and meek,
Deeply sensed and conveyed,
But never weak.

It can refresh from the grind of life's troublesome way,
Or renew your spirit at the end of the day.

My love can be so many things for you,
Clean and pure like the morning dew.
Or hot and steamy like an afternoon shower,
It can quench your cravings with its sheer power.

So, my love, I want to be
The everything you want in me.
I'll be your companion in good times and bad,
Your friend to share joys and comfort in sad.

Whatever the role you need at the moment.
I believe my love is that component.
So, since our days together seem too few,
I pray for a lifetime to share with you.

CHERISH

My heart aches in grief and
My soul cries in despair.
I search for a a glimpse of your face,
Or to hear your voice somewhere.

Just a glimmer of hope.
A simple smile or word,
Enough to sustain my soul,
Just enough to be heard.

Why do I continue to mourn
For those moments we are apart?
What is it that compels my yearning?
Why does your absence so prick my heart?

Is what we have so deep a love
That our hearts have become bound as one?
Or is my obsession rooted in selfishness,
Losing focus, for the truth to shun?

But, if selfishness, would I ever care
To emancipate you from a broken heart?
The suffering you endure, from avaricious indulgence,
Tears my soul apart.

But the desire to sacrifice, without recompense,
To give away for nothing in return,
Is not that heart the essence of love?
When joy compels sorrow to burn?

From, the well of my heart, true love overflows
Gushing forth in a life-giving flow.
A desire to give you all that is good,
Without regard for consequence or show.

Thus, I know that I love you,
Without question or doubt.
I will love you in wealth and
I will love you without.

Without concern for naught that I may receive,
Without hidden motive or any selfish thought to sever,
My heart and soul belong completely to you,
And I will cherish you forever.

GODLY FRIENDS

A loving friendship is eternal
When you have shared your heart.
There's no power in Heaven or on earth
That can tear that friendship apart.

Not distance nor time nor space
Can quench the agape spirit of a true friend.
The roots of that friendship grow far too strong
To be broken or even made to bend.

Together, we have shared tears of joy and of pain,
We have mourned broken hearts, celebrated marriage and birth,
But no human concept could ever measure
The infinite value of our friendship's worth.

Your future is paved by a road known to God,
And in His Mighty Hands you are secure.
He has given to you a living faith
And by His grace you shall endure.

Thank you for your timeless love,
Your patience, your graciousness and thought.
I will always remember with a song in my heart
The friendship that to us God has brought.

CHAPTER TWO
ROMANCE

ROMANCE

1. Clumsy Me | 55
2. A Single Rose | 56
3. An Intimate Kiss | 58
4. Love Built by Distance | 59
5. The Mortality of Love | 60
6. Truth | 61
7. Forever Quenched | 63
8. The Key to the Heart | 65
9. The Pain of Indifference | 69
10. When Two Hearts Connect | 71
11. The Deception of the Heart | 72
12. Places in the Heart | 75
13. Our Love | 76
14. An Offer of Love | 78
15. Forgiveness | 80
16. Just to Say I Love You | 83
17. The Tie That Binds | 84
18. A Resting Place | 86
19. Infinite Love? | 87
20. The Heart of a Man | 89
21. Never Another | 91
22. Love's Compelling Declaration | 93
23. The Measure of Love | 94
24. Light | 96
25. My Angel | 97

CLUMSY ME

Sometimes I get so clumsy,
I guess I cannot lie.
I slip, I trip, I stumble,
I fall and then I sigh.
But this time, it's been different.
I haven't seen a bruise.
I haven't even seen a scratch,
I haven't been confused.
But this fall was so dramatic,
Unexpected, unprepared and deep,
I never saw it coming,
Even though the slide was steep.
I couldn't catch myself from falling,
I couldn't do a thing.
I felt completely helpless,
Like a stone shot from a sling.
The power overwhelmed me,
It was futile to resist.
Like the steel drawn to the magnet,
I could not cease or desist.
No, this time, like no other,
There was no advance preview,
This fall which took me by surprise
Was when I fell in love with you.

A SINGLE ROSE

I wanted to leave you a single rose,
For the beauty I see in your face,
To remind you of how I adore you,
How I admire your elegance and grace.

But the rose, alone, could not convey my love.
Its fragrance, compared to you, was never so sweet.
I considered finding a whole rose garden,
So I searched up and down every street.

Yet though I discovered many glorious gardens,
With fragrance and beauty indeed,
In you I find so much more,
something else then I would need.

But what symbol could I give you,
To tell you all in my heart?
How could I ever convey that
I want us never to part?

Does any tangible thing convey such love,
Or describe the joy my heart celebrates
Every time I search into your eyes,
And feel the opening of love's flood gate?

No, forgive my failure to find, my love
Any tangible article to symbolize
The passion I hold in my heart for you
And the love I find in your eyes.

So, no flower nor jewel,
No diamond nor pearl
Not any precious stone,
Nor any treasures of this world,

Could compare to the beauty I see in your eyes,
Nor are any as worthy as your heart's cries.
Longing to express the passion of your soul,
Yearning to find the love which will make me whole.

Not an object of art,
No marble nor canvas,
Are as deep or as passionate
As what love hands us.

So as you go through this very day
Though our paths may even sever,
Remember how much I love you
And I will, always and forever.

AN INTIMATE KISS

Man knows no intimacy like a passionate kiss,
Blending of the mouths in heavenly bliss.
The touching of cheeks against one another,
Tightly closed eyes, eyelashes flutter,
While hands can display touch soft under cover,
And sensual words from tender voices utter.
There's nothing more intimate than an ardent kiss,
The ebb and flow of fervent pitch,
While hearts melt together, bodies ravage,
Energy dispersing so raw, almost savage.
There's nothing more intimate than a fervent kiss,
Desire transcendent, manners dismiss.
Confessions of yearning in eternal wish,
Tongues intertwining, a heavenly glimpse.
There's nothing more intimate than a feverish kiss,
Burning hunger and craving deep in the soul,
Love's desperation aspiring to control, while
Lips gently grasping, for joy to reminisce.
There's nothing more intimate than a frantic kiss,
Impulsive pining, too erotic to resist.
Sensuality prevailing, too late to restrain,
No care to abstain,
No concern to constrain.

LOVE BUILT BY DISTANCE

"Absence makes the heart grow fonder,"
A writer once has penned.
If his statement indeed is true,
On what does this depend?
Does this mean appreciation grows
Simply between two friends?
Or does it mean the heart will ache,
From a deep love that transcends?
Is it odd to believe the breaking of a heart
Can create love more intense?
For why would distance nourish a love
And not erect a defense?
Would not the heart seek to protect itself
Against painful regret?
Would not the heart, by its very nature,
Avoid foolish pretense?
Or perhaps does love's craving well up inside
Like a volcano bursting forth?
Can the heart then seek to hide
Love's internal source?
For that which springs from pressure,
Pressure that distance builds,
Is finally displayed like a treasure—
For then is the heart fulfilled.

THE MORTALITY OF LOVE

Will a love ever die a natural death?
Will it expire or simply lose its breath?
Can love die from emotional suffocation,
Deprived of spiritual inspiration?
Can love fade away from emotional malnutrition?
Wasting into oblivion without preservation?
Does not love demand its own air to breathe?
Does love not atrophy from emotional disease?
For love is not static, it must grow or decline,
It cannot remain still within purpose divine.
Yet love can be infected, for living is its design.
All animated infirmity with it are entwined.
Love produces its own fruits,
Blossom from the vine.
But if the vine is burned,
Is its fruit then also maligned?
Hatred and neglect are its perennial foes,
For these will sicken and halt all growth.
Hatred is poisonous air to the heart,
Death and sickness will it always impart.
But neglect, mere neglect,
far worse the nemesis,
destroys painfully and slowly,
Transforming the heart expresionless.

TRUTH

Does absolute truth truly exist?
Or is truth a variable concept?
Is truth a mere image reflected in a mirror?
Dependent on the viewer's object?
For if it were concrete, then how could it be
That each viewer's percept is different to see?
Or does the viewer alter the sight
By bending and even distorting its light?
Can truth become so hard to bear,
Black and white so distinct to compare,
That in pure light one cannot dare
To look upon truth with fervent stare?
Is a man's heart black or white?
Is it dark or is it bright?
Does the heart disfigure truth's sight
To soften the blow
By warping the light?
For if absolute truth were present in mind,
Then what inevitable impact is there to find?
How then would the truth govern the heart?
What altering mandate would it impart?
Would agitation and pain then appear?
Perhaps the light must then alter to steer?
Else is the distress much too clear?
Else is the anguish much too sheer?

So if absolute truth truly exists,
Will a man ever venture to see
That cognitive dissonance that will grow
And blossom from the root of truth's tree?
Or will he in fear run and hide
In him the truth never to abide?
For the torture he rejects and rescinds,
Never allowing to entertain the chagrin,
The truth that must alter, amend and transform
His nature construe, his will to conform.

FOREVER QUENCHED?

Once that flame has burned out,
Can it ever again find its spark?
Will it ever again brighten its corner,
Or is it destined to die in the dark?
Has that flame lost its glow,
Never again to be reborn?
Will its aroma again with sweetness
Saturate perhaps and adorn?
Or has it become extinguished,
No warmth again to share?
For when that flame flickers out,
What fuel can make it flare?
How can some mysterious torch
Miraculously bring it light?
Is it now ordained surrender,
Finished is its fight?
So why then does a heart struggle,
Battle and exert,
To rekindle a flame once quenched,
From the subtle to the overt?
Why is that hope eternal,
Springing forth within the breast?
Why does the gradual ember's death
untimely trigger distress?
When should a heart renounce

that a fire once so pure,
has dwindled and died out,
for which there is no cure?
Is there fault to be blamed
Is the flame seized in its prison?
Or is the outcome still the same,
Regardless of the villain?

THE KEY TO THE HEART

Men search their entire lifetimes
For the key to fit a lock,
Yearning, craving, seeking,
While time's hands run a dwindling clock.
The struggle offers answers,
Money, wealth and power,
All purport to turn the key.
But each will the heart devour.
For none of these can fill the soul,
None truly satisfy.
Not money, wealth or power,
Can ever gratify.
Each one is a perpetual fraud,
Blinding the heart's sight and vision.
Each of them inherently flawed,
Binding the heart in eternity's prison.
For the heart is the ephemeral core
Of the nature of mankind,
It cannot be filled by those things
That most men strive to find.
Within the heart created is an empty well for more,
The answer must run deep enough
For the key to open that door.
Men innately know the answer,
Yet impatiently they ignore,

Settling for simplistic,
Unwilling to explore.
But the answer is never on the surface,
It lies within the depth,
When one heart finds another
And infuses love's true breath.

THE PAIN OF INDIFFERENCE

Is there rationale for the human heart's condition?
How is it adept at both despising and at passion?
Perhaps its emotions even defy definition,
Does it thus elude parameter and impaction?
For hate has its certain content of revile,
Whether small or great,
It will surely the heart defile.
And love exudes its measure of zeal,
Sometimes consuming the soul,
Or even superficial, yet real.
But indifference by nature is a vacuum of guile,
Possessing neither loathing nor nurture,
Yet to the dependent hostile.
For apathy is devoid of all soul's emotion,
Emptied of all hatred,
Devoid of all devotion.
Embodied by its nature of absolute frigidity,
Empathy having died by erosion,
Passion having failed its test of validity.
So which agony is inherently most intense?
That which love causes,
Either shallow or dense?
Or that of hate, negative passion,
Yet a known false pretense,
And still love's assassin?

Or is indifference the evil saboteur?
Indifference, that which eludes comprehension,
Desolate and barren,
Having its own undefinable dimension.
Soulless, complacent and callous at best,
Neither hot nor cold,
And yet tepid and repressed.

WHEN TWO HEARTS CONNECT

When two hearts truly connect,
The fireworks blaze into space,
The violins play their sweet melody,
The drums beat the thump of the bass.
When two hearts truly connect,
A shooting star crosses the horizon.
Flares from the sun warm the globe,
The clouds disappear into oblivion,
When two hearts truly connect,
The stars don't really align,
No the universe doesn't notice,
There's no miraculous sign.
When two hearts truly connect,
Only those hearts truly know.
But in their deepest regions,
An ember begins to glow.
And that ember will blaze into a rage,
For a love that burns to be shown,
Unless those hearts extinguish that flame,
Its nature will flourish, consume.
Until love fuses those hearts into one,
The fire will burn out the gloom.
But whether that fire becomes an inferno,
Whether loves basks in its glow,
Hearts have choices that they must make,
Only those hearts truly know.

THE DECEPTION OF THE HEART

If love never fails,
If love endures all things,
If love is always kind,
If love patience brings,
Then how can love bring anguish?
How can it cause pain?
Or is a heart so selfish
That love is truly vain?
Is that which we call love
A counterfeit, not real?
So perhaps true love must
Be more than what we feel?
But true love must have emotion
It must involve the heart;
The heart alone has passion,
Devotion to impart.
The heart alone creates courage,
Without there's no resolve.
Sometimes a heart defies reason,
Where logic doesn't solve,
But isn't that what life fulfills,
Fantasy as the toll?
For without the passion of the heart,
Does living possess a soul?

So does true love defy human existence?
Does it transcend humanity's nature?
Is its purity by nature resistant?
Or is genuine love something greater ?

PLACES IN THE HEART

Every memory is a room,
The heart is the memory's home,
Each room filled with emotion,
Some rooms are joyful,
Some cold as stone.
Some rooms store occasions,
Festivals and parties enjoyed,
Others store tragedies,
Pain and heartbreaks to avoid.
Some rooms hold feelings
Of loves held and lost,
Others hold anger from
Inequities and passions tossed.
Each of us live in these rooms,
Dwelling therein all our days.
And these rooms continue to fill,
where we make the choice to stay.
Do we choose to live in the rooms
Where pain and tragedy prevail?
Or do we choose to live in the rooms
Where joy, jubilation avail?
For where we stay will proliferate
The memories stored in that room,
And where we avoid will dissipate
Or that room will be our tomb.

OUR LOVE

I do not understand our love—
Especially why and how.
But beyond a shadow of a doubt,
I deeply love you now.

I could never deny it, or even suggest,
You have captured the core of my soul.
From the very moment I first heard your voice,
I knew that you'd make me whole.

I've met many people throughout my life,
And I can truthfully gauge
There is no other person on the face of the earth
With your passion and gift to encourage.

You're God's gift to the world of loneliness,
His design to uplift the disturbed.
And I know from the depth of my very soul
That you can revive with just a word.

So I cannot fathom why you'd ever love me,
I feel so unworthy; but rather,
I am grateful to our majestic Creator
That our hearts have found each other.

On this day of expression,
I could not help but write
This poem prepared for your soul,
How your love has given me sight,

Not physical sight with which to see
For with my eyes I have beheld your beauty.
But sight of the soul, from which is revealed
Truth, virtue and duty.

The love and passion here in my heart
For you will never change or diminish.
I assuredly promise it will merely deepen,
It will never end, conclude or finish.

I sense what I hold in my heart for you
Is unconditional, eternal and rare.
And for that reason I can boldly declare
That to love you is my lifelong prayer.

AN OFFER OF LOVE

My love for you is higher than the world's highest peak;
It's deeper than the deepest sea.
It will ever last, through any violent storm,
For it will ever be.

This love, so tightly entwined in my heart,
Is more natural than any I've known.
It will never fail, not wither nor die,
Its roots will deepen and grow.

I cannot convey, for words always falter,
What I hold here in my heart.
But I trust my soul's longing, its yearning, its plea
It's desire that we never part.

Please never reject the purity of my love,
For the soul from which it derives
Has waited an eternity to express
This rare love which transcends so many lives.

This love can be bruised and damaged, to be sure.
It may even be mortally defaced.
But like the one from whom our love originates,
It will prevail and, despite all, will be raised.

No matter what the future may hold,
Whether we are ever united or not,
Though our love may stumble and even fall,
I cannot rescind what I have so long sought.

Please accept the worth of my love,
Whether you can return or impart.
Know that I expect nothing in return—
That truth alone will fill my heart.

FORGIVENESS

I know at times I falter.
I fail and sometimes hurt you.
I know that I'm not faultless—
I'm only human, yes it's true.

I know sometimes I'm anxious,
Even nervous, maybe testy.
I'm sure I can be moody,
And my many calls are pesty.

But through all the trial,
Tribulation, storms and even wave,
I hope that you'll forgive me,
It's your love I'll always crave.

Through your tender, kind compassion,
You have taught me love that's real,
Not a fake or artificial kind,
That people so often steal.

But a love that is genuine—
Nothing fake and never selfish.
Ne'er before have I known love like this,
It's deep, whole and rich.

For even if the sky
Were a parchment or a scroll—
And if the seas were made of ink,
I could never write the whole,

To describe the depth of my love for you
Would exceed the deepest ocean.
Its height would reach beyond the stars
Its breadth beyond the heavens.

So, forgive me when I don't act loving,
Or when I'm impatient or hurried.
For my love for you will not falter,
Even though I might seem worried.

I miss you when you are away.
I feel it when you fret.
Even though you may try to hide it.
I know when you're upset.

Our souls and hearts have found each other—
And a match they certainly are.
For time and eternity may pass away
And distance may separate us afar.

But our hearts will always feel their mates—
Regardless of time or space.
And the love that grows inside those hearts
Will bring us face to face.

For the link between our souls is firm.
It's a bond that is strong and secure.
So no matter what we confront,
Our love will forever endure.

JUST TO SAY "I LOVE YOU"

I just wanted to find a special way
To say you're on my mind,
Some words to say "I love you"
And that, in you, I find
new meaning for the word "love",
New places in my heart,
Revived again from their dormant state
Like a masterpiece of art.
Your mind, your heart, your boundless love
Are gifts indeed to be treasured,
And to know you have given them to me
Staggers my unworthy heart as unmeasured.
Remember each day that I love you,
That you are my lifetime dream—
And that without your passion,
Your kindness in endless stream,
I am a man without hope, without purpose,
Lost in a world of pain,
For I need your love to make me whole,
You are my everything.

THE TIE THAT BINDS

Is there a time when love it too little?
For if it is real, can it be that brittle?
If love is true, is it a fortress?
A barrier, stronghold, without is it worthless?
So many say " love," but
Do they sense what they mean?
Is the word mere triviality?
For feelings yet unseen?
Is the word a mere cliché?
Letters to fill a space,
Nothing deep intended,
So easy to erase!
Or does the word purvey weight immortal?
Anticipation involving the mind?
For to withstand life's unknown portals,
Are truth and devotion so hard to find?
Without them, from whence comes love's fiber?
The sinew to cement and unite?
Without them, what else can serve
To create a binding so tight?
For won't emotions waft with the tide?
Easily tossed to and fro?
No solid rock for the storm,
foundation for the high and the low.
Then what will secure in the tempest,

Some harbor, some rescue from flood?
Or will the deluge overwhelm,
Destroy and bury in life's mud?
How then will love survive?
What structure must exist,
For love to endure the test,
For a love to further persist?

A RESTING PLACE

The mind must have a place to dwell,
A place that seems its home.
A place to which it may retreat
From wherever it may roam.
A place where it pleasure brings,
Where it may find its ease.
A place where peace and love abound,
Where its rest may be appeased.
The mind must find its peace
Somewhere in the heart,
Where truth and passion reside serene,
In the crossroad where they meet.
Where conflict no longer lives,
Where their struggle finds defeat.
A place where the heart is satisfied,
Where harmony is complete.
A place where pain has lost its grip,
Where joy fulfills and gratifies,
A place where discord cannot abide,
A place where ideals can fantasize.
Does such a place truly exist?
Or it the ideal of utopia
Mere fiction existing only in dreams,
Or is reality truly dystopia?

INFINITE LOVE ?

If it's truth that love endures all things,
Then can it ever end?
Why does it sometime disappear?
Or was that just pretend?
For if love is living and breathing,
Should it not adversity transcend?
If love has life beyond human comprehension,
On what does its life depend?
For if a love is combatted indeed,
Then how deeply can it descend?
Does depth not inspire a stronger bond,
Against tribulation to defend?
The heart of a man has facets unknown;
They can celebrate and condemn.
The heart is leery and fearful of pain
So barriers for protection attend.
But when the heart's struggle repels a love,
How deeply can love extend?
For if that love cannot take root
In the deep ground of the heart,
Will not the storms invade and destroy,
And tear a love apart?
Then what happens to that love,
Is it still there or does it depart?
Did that love simply vanish,

Like an ice cube in the sun?
Or did that love slowly decay,
As if it had never begun?

THE HEART OF A MAN

The heart of a man should be an open book.
Filled with memories,
Flowing gently like a brook.
The heart of a man should rely on truth,
Honest in conversation,
Learned in days of youth.
The heart of a man should seek integrity,
Virtuous in its values,
Acting not selfishly.
The heart of a man should strive to be pure,
Minimizing lurid thoughts,
Rejecting their allure.
The heart of a man was designed for love,
Passion not in hatred,
Descending from above.
But can the heart of man achieve this purity?
Can the heart ever reach such maturity?
Or is the heart by nature
Envious and cruel?

To assume a heart is purified,
Will that make one a fool?
Or is life more fulfilling to
Accept purity presumed?
Will joy truly flow from the heart
When this naivete consumes?

NEVER ANOTHER

There are many things in life
I just can't understand—
Like the beauty of a distant star
Or how it excites to touch your hand.

Why my tongue fails to find the right words
When I ponder my love for you.
How I instinctively know that our love
Is so ever rare and true.

Yet though I may not understand
What creates our intense passion but rather,
I know that such a passion as ours
I can and will never share with another.

So please forgive me for this little poem
Which comes straight from my heart—
But the notion destroys me when I consider
That we may one day be apart.

No matter whether we share all we have,
As I so dream and wish,
Just to gaze on you at a stolen moment in time
Will surpass the joy of any other's kiss.

For even if we may share
A mere fragment of our affection,
Twill be more gratifying than to bestow my all
Upon any other or in any direction.

I cannot deny that there may be other friends
With whom I could laugh or smile.
But never will there be any other
For your heart is my domicile.

Please understand this pronouncement,
My heart's declaration of poise,
It is neither a slave to your love nor captive
But rather sullened by its compelling choice.

It is not that you have stolen my heart
but rather, to you, I have given,
for the eyes of my soul see only you,
so to your heart I am driven.

And what I have given to you
I cannot now dissolve.
For my heart is forever yours,
By my decision, my choice, my resolve.

LOVE'S COMPELLING DECLARATION

True love's never easy,
Hard to find and hard to keep.
At times it brings you ecstasy,
At others makes you weep.

But true love when, once found,
Its power so devout,
Your heart wants to whisper to every soul,
From the mountaintops to shout.

Imitations and counterfeits may abound,
But true love is so rare,
That the very fibers of your soul
Yearn to bow in gracious prayer.

For when a life of searching is climaxed in passion,
The atunement of a soul to its mate,
The heart is compelled to declare its joy
For at last it has fulfilled its fate.

So I do not believe one can ignore true love,
Unlike the counterfeits set aside.
For can the heart of one's soul, its life driving force,
From its rejuvenating desire hide?

THE MEASURES OF LOVE

How do I love thee? Let me count the ways.

The glow of your radiant smile will entice me all my days.

The penetrating passion from your dark sensual eyes

Prompts my heart to leap so frantic

your presence ever to be craved,

delirium so dramatic.

The tender touch of your compassionate caress

Can calm my soul and soothe it to rest.

And your body, its ever so perfect form

Sparks my intrigue and keeps me ever warm.

I love thee in more ways than I can tell,

Countless as the stars,

Higher than the heavens,

Deeper than the deepest hell.

No rose possesses a fragrance so sweet,

Nor its blossoms such beauty can hold

As the splendor I see when I gaze into your face,

Such a story could never be told.

For I love thee more than tongue can speak

Or mortal mind could conceive.

Greater still than all human kind could imagine

More than hearts will ever believe.

LIGHT

Your love brightens the path I tread.
Your warmth shines through the shadows of my darkest night.
You cause me to penetrate the murky dread,
Where once I was blind, you give me sight.

Without your love, I am hopelessly lost
In a world which never forgives.
Without your compassion, I'd be helplessly tossed,
With no reason to continue to live.

You are the wings on which I soar
To heights that I'd never known.
Your love has permeated my very core
And without you, I'm perpetually alone.

You are the key to the love in my heart,
Which unlocks passion's well spring of hope
And it seems that I knew from the very start
That your love would bring me the will to cope.

You have the gift of encouragement
And I am grateful to God for your love
For I know that you are an angel,
Just to share with me from above.

MY ANGEL

She hasn't any wings,
Or a halo that glows.
Though her voice is soft and sweet,
She rarely speaks with celestial prose.

Her face has beauty unsurpassed,
But her body still requires sleep.
And even though heaven is her eternal home,
Today she resides where she is able to weep.

She doesn't wear a long flowing gown,
Or even play a harp.
But she sings with tenderness, passion and care,
Like the gentle voice of the lark.

No, she wasn't created without a free will,
But she rarely thinks of herself first.
She never delivered to man the message of God's word,
But she knows it chapter and verse.

I guess that, in truth,
She's not an angel from above,
But I still adore and worship her
And I give her all of my love.

For never before, in the history of this world,
Has there been a woman,
More rare than a perfect pearl,
Whose beauty of heart was so deep and pure,
So I am certain it will ever endure.

So, in closing, I concede that God's angel
I know she cannot be,
But I also know deep in my heart,
She is always an angel to me.

CHAPTER THREE
THE BROKEN HEART

THE BROKEN HEART

1. Heart Cry | 103
2. If | 105
3. Pain | 106
4. The Purpose of the Heart | 107
5. The Masks We Wear | 109
6. The Yearnings of the Heart | 113
7. Too Late | 114
8. When a Heart's Been Broken | 116
9. Walls | 119
10. The Cruelty of Indifference | 121
11. The Lily | 125
12. Repairing a Shattered Heart | 127
13. Truth in Deceit | 129
14. Trusting God | 131
15. Trust | 132
16. Motives of the Heart | 133
17. The Wellspring of Motive | 135
18. Alone | 136
19. Justice in Love? | 138
20. The Heart Can be Evil | 140
21. Missing in Action | 141

HEART CRY

Is it a whisper, a shout,
or a soft quiet voice?
Is it heard only in the mind,
Inside the soul,
Does it offer a choice?
Can it be heard when it shatters,
Or is it merely felt?
Is it sensed for the moment,
Is it lasting,
Does the pain ever melt?
Is it steady when it hurts,
Does it diminish or increase?
Are there moments the sting strikes,
Does It attach,
Does it release?
How deeply does it penetrate,
Near the surface,
Or to the core?
Will there ever be a peace,
A calm,
Or does it remain at war?
For there will be lows,
There will be highs,
Some triggers are expected,
But others will surprise.

Yet it is the anguish
that may never subside,
That may cut like a knife
Deep down inside,
The tears that may fall and
Yet vary in size,
Are passion's remorse
When a broken heart cries.

IF

If love never betrays,
If love is eternal,
IF love tenderness portrays,
If love is supernal,
If love is patient,
If love never self serves,
If love is gracious, and
If love life preserves,
Then why does love cause pain?
Why is love despondent?
Why is love so often feigned?
How then can love falter?
How then can love be slain?
There must exist the illusion;
That which cannot be achieved.

PAIN

Which pain hurts the deepest,
That of the body or the heart?
From which does a person recover,
Which will quickly depart?
The body usually heals itself,
A miracle indeed.
But the anguish of the heart
Perpetuates its bleed.
A wounded body may heal with scars,
And its function may be impaired,
But the heart can rarely love the same,
For its passion is never repaired.
The mind may fear and distrust,
Trepidation may appear,
But the heart's fear of loving
Will make purpose disappear.
For to love is endemic to why the heart exists.
And if panic dispels that purpose,
Then its failure inevitably persists.
So which anguish cuts the deepest?
That to the body or the heart?
Which will heal but which will not?
So which pain will never depart?

THE PURPOSES OF THE HEART

If the heart is desperately wicked,
As so stated in the Word,
Then why was it created,
Or is its purpose truly absurd?
Does it contravene existence,
Perform contrary to the real?
If its function is truly evil,
Then should we never feel?
But isn't it true that emotion
creates that very spark,
The ember that burns life's satisfaction,
That brings light into the dark?
For joy and sadness,
While opposing as an adversary,
Are the passions that we seek,
Fulfillment that they carry,
Whether strong or weak.
For is not black darker
When compared to white?
Do we know the day's sunlight
From its following the night?
Without the heart,
Would we even know
How our days can fulfill us,
Truth that passions show?

Or would time be mere existence,
Gratification foreign to our minds?
Satisfaction non existent,
To which our minds are blind?

THE MASKS WE WEAR

Shakespeare once called all life a stage,
and we are all players in it.
Is his assertion truth?
or is his assertion fiction?
Do we all search for the perfect mask?
Do we all portray an image?
Do we strive to conceal the truth?
To alter our soul's very visage?
Why do we yearn for other's approval,
To even betray the heart?
Disguise the truth of what's inside,
Honesty to conceal, not impart?
Is it a fear we cannot articulate?
And what influence gives it such might?
To pacify this fear, we cover with veils
Replace the blind for the sight!
We camouflage, conceal and hide
Our hearts' deepest desires.
Securing the truth deep inside,
External conversion to liars.

Why must we portray for others to see
Prevarications, falsehoods, fairy tales?
Is the honest truth shame for what lies inside?
Conception the truth will fail?
So how long must we wear our masks?
Covering up the heart's truest pining?
Always striving to appease others' whims,
The heart rarely aligning?
What result if we strip off the masks?
Longing for change in its place,
Change the heart to find its peace?
Truth then to embrace?

YEARNINGS OF THE HEART

I never saw it coming,
But like a snowball down the hill
I could not stop its momentum,
It overcame my will.
Sometimes a beating heart's passion
Is more powerful than one might plan.
Like a magnet drawn to metal,
A woman and a man.
The force of love is mystery,
But its strength cannot be denied.
More endurance than nature itself,
From which one cannot easily hide.
Yet when quandary pervades,
How can one resolve?
The heart craves sensual fulfillment,
But the mind demands reproof.
Is frustration the prevailing answer?
Is such a solution there to part?
So how to reach and satisfy
The yearnings of the heart?

TOO LATE

The crevasse of my heart was dark;
It was empty, it was quiet.
No sounds did it emit,
No voice did it acquire.
Was that heart alive or dead?
My mind wondered in lifeless peace.
For nothing in it long had stirred,
All feeling had come to cease.
Long ago had it resigned
To live without a mission.
It seemed that joy had made its exit,
Now its lasting condition.
Struggle as it had to find
That magic life giving elixir,
But rejection had long replaced
Rejuvenation's fixture.
The one to whom life had been given
Became the devil's toy,
Drawing each breath from this heart
With wisdom and stealth so coy.
Until life had given way
To a sad and relentless death,
This heart succumbing finally
Surrendering its last breath.

Is resurrection conceivable?
Can this heart breathe once again?
Or is it relegated to lie in the tomb?
Now it's eternal domain.

WHEN A HEART'S BEEN BROKEN

When a heart's been broken,
Love's clock stops keeping time,
Its hands no longer move ahead.
Its silent bell won't chime.
The joy that once billowed forth,
Like a fountain bursting flood,
Recedes to a mere trickle,
Its jubilation now succumbs.
The vivid colors its garden adorned
Have dulled and lost their shimmer,
No longer does the light of day
Bring forth luminescent glimmer.
The melody that once had played,
that heralded love's sweet tune,
has suddenly become quiet,
love's song is now immune.
The love that once the soul enlivened
Has surrendered and taken captive
That myriad of sensual purpose
Now vacant and inactive.

WALLS

How can a heart be broken,
Shattered too deeply to feel?
Once fragmented beyond understanding,
Is there any hope it will heal?
For only love has the power indeed
To render such pain,
create fear of its need.
Only love can cause a heart to implode,
To wipe away emotion,
Its passion erode.
Only love derives dismay from its gift,
Only love can set the soul adrift.
Lost in the sea of love's tumultuous tempest,
To what kind of a love
must this heart then be destined?
Is there any greater blessing a man can give
Than that of his heart,
But such anguish to risk?
So once broken and shattered in pieces,
Will he give it again,
Or set barriers against breeches?
Barriers that will secure against pain,
Agony, desperation, from love to abstain?
Can those walls ever be broken?
For the greater the pain, the deeper the passion,

The more fortified the walls, the firmer their traction.
The agony arises the greater the gift,
For it is in the giving so deep,
Which intensifies love's conflict.
Experience is the teacher,
For a lesson grievously learned,
The walls provide protection,
So can love ever return?

THE CRUELTY OF INDIFFERENCE

Is there rationale for the human heart's condition?
Why Is it adept at both despising and at passion?
Perhaps its emotions even defy definition,
Does it thus elude parameter and impaction?
For hate has its certain content of revile,
Whether small or great,
It will surely the heart defile.
And Love exudes its measure of zeal,
Sometimes consuming the soul,
Or even superficial, yet real.
But indifference by nature is a vacuum of guile,
Possessing neither loathing nor nurture,
Yet to the dependent hostile.
For apathy is devoid of all soul's emotion,
Emptied of all hatred
Yet missing all devotion.
Embodied by its nature of absolute frigidity,
Empathy having died by erosion,
Passion having failed its test of validity.
So which agony is inherently most intense?
That which love causes,
Either shallow or dense?
Or that of hate, negative passion,
Yet a known false pretense,
And still love's assassin?

Or is indifference the evil saboteur?
Indifference, that which eludes comprehension,
Desolate and barren,
Having its own dimension.
Soulless, complacent and callous at best,
Neither hot nor cold,
And yet tepid and repressed.

THE LILY

Of all the flowers in the field
The lily is a favorite indeed.
Graceful, elegant and fragrant,
It starts as a simple seed.
To grow, the lily needs sunshine,
Light and warmth to absorb.
For the sun prospers an array of colors,
Dark and cold are abhorred.
The colors reflect the lily's strength,
Brightness being its true character.
Red, yellow, orange or white,
Even the pink and lavender.
The bulb must be planted in a place
Where water absorbs in the ground.
Water will strengthen the lily's roots,
But too much and the lily will drown.
The temperature cannot be frigid,
Though a slight chill will seal it unique.
So the lily can bloom and blossom,
Most beautiful in the boutique.
A lily never becomes dormant,
Growth perpetual to death.
So the lily must continue to flourish
So long as it has breath.
For without the right ingredients,

A lily cannot survive,
And because it never can sleep,
Only growth will keep it alive.
Once the lily has passed, however,
Can it revive again?
Can the lily return to seed?
Can it resurrected life attain?
Or has its cycle ended,
After cultivation has long been ignored?
Only then regret to prevail,
The lily's demise thus assured?

REPAIRING A SHATTERED HEART

If a heart in shards is shattered,
Will it ever mend?
If the pieces are fractured and splintered,
How crushed can those fragments distend?
To what depth are the shards of pain
The heart must seek to repair?
Distending to what levels so deep,
The sheer degree of despair?
Does it depend on the skill of the
One to whom the repair must fall?
The one who has a sensitive touch,
A love on which to call?
For a heart, once shattered, is damaged inside
And cannot its own remedy make.
Another with love to altruistically share,
For passion and love alone's sake,
Must reach in and align the shattered pieces
Of the heart that has fallen apart.
For only then can joy enter in and
Seal the pieces of that heart.

For without that seal, will the heart beat again?
Can a wounded bird take flight?
Can the Andrea Doria ever sail again?
Can a blinded man find sight?
Does the seal not create the bonding
Of the fragments of that fractured heart?
So what joy is the seal that heals the wounds?
What strength does it impart?
But even sealed must not the heart
survive with lasting scars?
Scars that outline every pain,
Wounds from every war.
For if once shattered, pieces may rejoin,
But will they ever love the same?
For can a heart once shattered
create sonic rhythm again?
Can it reignite love's flame?

TRUTH IN DECEIT

You refused to trust my words
Though they are as true as any could be.
I have poured my very heart to you,
In truth and transparency so free.

I love you with all that is in me,
I have tried to show you in so many ways.
I have given you my very heart and my soul.
And I will love you all of my days.

No, I am not as flawless as you suppose,
I do err in words and in speech.
But I urge you to explore your own soul,
And to find the love in mine in your reach.

For when you search beyond the frailty of my words
And grasp the purity of their source,
You will find that I have tried to express
The complete truth, in honesty and course.

I cannot let go of what we have had,
Our love that seemed so pure and rare.
And no matter how far I may search,
I will find never another to compare.

Though I acknowledge my errors of the past,
My sins of fault, I do admit.
Yet I struggle to find the reason for your mistrust,
For no wrong did I commit.

I have tussled in vain to earn back your trust.
Through honesty and completeness so open.
Yet you reject me still, exploiting my flaw,
Destroying that which I had hope in.

But your reasons are beyond my grasp,
For I thought I knew your heart.
Have you deceived me? No, I reject that thought,
For I have loved you from the start.

So what reason could you have to strike down my love?
In truth, is it a lack of trust?
Or is there some other reason? A motive you may not even see?
That makes rationalizing rejection a must?

I know my words are not always right.
Even you know I make mistakes.
But my heart for you seeks not to deceive.
It conveys truth and never a fake.

Please do not throw away what we have
In exchange for a false belief of defeat,
For no greater loss could we ever endure,
Than discarding our trust for deceit.

TRUSTING GOD

I often think of you and cry,
My heart pours itself out and wonders why,
Is it an act of God or just cruel fate?
Was my love too early or just too late?

For you are the woman of my dreams,
And no matter how much I desire and scheme,
I cannot tell my soul a lie—
I know I will love you until I die.

For in your love, I have found
A love without restriction, condition or bound.
The intensity of our love so rare
Makes such a fate seem so unfair.

But I know that in God is a love and care
Greater than any we could ever share.
And if we place our trust in Him,
His promises He will fulfill within.

For He promises never to leave or forsake,
No matter what wrongs that we may make
And we know that His love will be ever true
So I know I can trust Him to take care of you.

TRUST

Once a heart has been fractured,
Can it learn to trust again?
Having felt the anguish that brings,
Will it risk hurt, and when?
To truly love deeply inside
And give the heart undisclosed,
Is the gift of ultimate vulnerability,
And leaves one's essence exposed.
For is there any greater gift
Than that of the very heart,
The ebb and flow of a life?
For what more can a man
give away and divulge
Than his very purposeful design?
Once then grievously betrayed,
how can a man once again
Give and disclose to that same
Risk of despair and when?
Is a man then perhaps better served
By purposeful sheer self-preservation
To hold back his heart completely,
In absolute reservation?
Or will that choice ultimately
Defy the heart's very creation?
Destining that heart to live
An empty and meaningless isolation?

MOTIVES OF THE HEART

Hard to understand are the motives of a man,
What lies underneath in the heart,
How much truth, how much lie,
What makes him laugh,
What makes him cry,
What builds him up,
And what tears him apart.
Stranger indeed the man to himself,
What is the wellspring of his conduct?
Does he understand his very own heart?
What will encourage and what will destruct?
Has he planted the seeds himself within?
Does he recognize their blossom?
Is all he can see what's above the ground,
Never beneath on the bottom?
Does his heart speak a language
he cannot comprehend?
Can he ever grasp its expression?
Does he know its tongue his life controls?
Both liberty and yet oppression?
But What if he knew how to cultivate
The garden's most majestic flower?
What if he could transplant its fruits
Before humanity's stormy encounter?
What then would sprout forth from

The garden of his heart?
Would weeds seek then to devour?
Or could beauty and serenity then prevail?
Could their colors so vivid and bright
eclipse the weeds of despair,
removing the blinders from its sight?
What seeds then would germinate,
Permeate and by their nature expand?
What allure of the heart would then be exposed?
If we could change the motives of a man?

THE WELLSPRING OF MOTIVE

Does a man understand his own motivations?
Does he know how to lie to himself?
Can he interpret his true aspirations?
Is he selfless or do his words dispel?
For if a man were true to his own mind,
Admitting the depths of his heart,
Could he then ever judge another,
If so, must truth fade and depart?
"There but by the grace of God," is common
And it's wisdom familiar to most.
But the truth that a man ignores in his heart
Necessarily becomes integrity's ghost.
Fault and evil are the offspring of self,
Innately composing its song,
But self is the wellspring of motive,
The source of all that is wrong.
Can the flow of that well be changed,
Can its tainted water become pure?
Can that flow become true and sweet,
Can it become that which it abhors?
Or is its current fixed in the stream
Which gave to it its birth?
Or is it destined to endure
its own begotten worth?

ALONE

There is no pain like feeling alone,
It tears at the soul.
It's as cold as a stone.
But when the one you love
Has so suddenly departed,
The loneliness you feel
Renders you broken hearted.
The emptiness and void
That you sense deep down inside
Is a vacuum of senselessness
That drains your passions dry.
You crave to taste, to feel, to touch,
And even love again.
But the spirit that dwells within the heart
—that shared by all men—
Rebels in compelled devotion
To reject, stand firm, defend.
Yet is loneliness from loss
Comparable to unity?
The heart yearns for passion's knot,
Yet in another arises mutiny.
Can that heart survive
The battle against its nature?

Or will its fount of flowing love
Trickle to self erasure?
For is love's flow independent,
Without need for a replenishing source?
Or will its sourceless flow finally parch,
Absent a rejuvenating course?

JUSTICE IN LOVE?

Your laughter and smile haunt my mind,
Of joyous times spent in your care,
Of a companionship never known before,
As I am compelled to ask, it is fair?

Fair to have ever known such love,
To have ever dared to believe—
That you could value such an unworthy man,
Yet, still, through memories I grieve.

I grieve the loss of a heart fulfilled—
Of a dream so fervently sought.
For could any other fill this heart's void—
Or is it whimsy which I have fought?

Was it foolish to have believed in the truth of love?
Can two hearts genuinely meet?
Or is what I perceived a cloak at best,
Surreal, just a shell, personified deceit?

Is love merely an elaborate illusion—
An invention of the mind and the will?
Can two souls truly give of themselves—
Binding their hearts in a lifelong seal?

Does an altruistic motive find truth in humanity,
Or is giving a disguise for its foe?
For if truth is in motive, the satisfaction of giving,
Is that not the same seed from which selfishness will grow?

So then, can love ever be giving—
In sacrifice, without recourse or gain?
Or does it undo itself, by sheer definition,
Declaring its existence in vain?

THE HEART CAN BE EVIL

The heart can be evil; the heart can be kind,
The heart can give freedom but the heart can also bind,
The heart can be gentle; the heart can be harsh.
The heart can open doors but it can also create bars.
The heart can find a pathway but it can also get lost;
The heart can be steady but it can also be tossed.
The heart can be peaceful, contented and warm.
But the heart can find turmoil, trouble and storm.
The heart is an enigma, no man truly knows.
But whatever it reaps derives from what it sows.
The product you see, the heart's very pulse,
Is nourished and grown by good or repulse.
If love is your desire for the heart's outward flow,
Then love must be that from which it would grow.
For if anger and evil are that which it consumes,
Then frustration and hate will be its natural bloom.

MISSING IN ACTION

The scars of many battles
Marred my body and soul
Twenty years of combat
Had finally taken its toll.

I had taken many a hill,
Charged the enemy at its line,
So the opposing army aimed its sights,
And the soul in its sight was mine.

After a long and arduous battle,
The body's weariness finally succumbed.
The enemy's flaming arrow
Penetrated my skin; and my soul went completely numb.

I was wounded more in my heart,
The body would soon repair.
But the scars my own troops were about to inflict
Were more than my soul could bear.

I was stranded on the battlefield,
No soldier came to my rescue.
They all fled my very presence,
I saw not a one, much less a few.

So I waited patiently for my deliverer,
Lying prostrate, facing the ground.
The burning pain from the enemy's attack
Rendered me helpless, weakened and bound.

Days turned to weeks and then weeks to months,
But a friendly face would never appear
So my heart grew weaker, sullened, discouraged,
And in torture, I shed many a tear.

Why was I forsaken
By those that I had led?
Did they expect that I was impervious?
That my wounds should not have bled?

Where were they— those, who for twenty years,
Had said they loved me so?
Had they just been playing a game?
Had they not learned to handle this blow?

Why were they so quick to judge—
To assess my own fault and blame?
Yet so slow to show me what they had professed,
How is THAT love, just the same?

Truly, where are their hearts?
Are they in love with the commander in chief?
Or rather, is their love committed to themselves,
In reality, is that their belief?

To what army do we give allegiance?
One which rescues, heals and more?
Or have we chosen to surrender the fallen,
Giving the enemy its prisoners of war?

Examine your heart and look at your soul—
Are you swift to judge and take sides?
Or is your love unconditional, liberating those
Who have been taken by the enemy's strides?

www.ingramcontent.com/pod-product-compliance
Lightning Source LLC
Chambersburg PA
CBHW060837170426
43192CB00019BA/2806